JOINING THE CHURCH

A Manual of Membership for Methodists

London
EPWORTH PRESS

© EPWORTH PRESS 1968
FIRST PUBLISHED IN 1968
BY EPWORTH PRESS
(Book Steward: Frank H. Cumbers)
SBN 7162 0018 X

Printed in Great Britain by
Strand Press Service Ltd.,
West Norwood S.E.27

Contents

Introduction

THIS Manual is not intended to be a complete guide to every issue that may be raised within a training course for Church members. It does not set out the precise contents for such a course, nor outline the proportions of time needed for the various essential features. Many matters are lightly touched upon here which will need fuller explanation and discussion (e.g. items in the Creed).

It is intended to be a summary of those matters which are of particular importance in this training, and to suggest an ordering of the material which will be educationally right. It attempts to look at the nature of Christian living, experience and faith in a way that makes sense both to a young person coming fresh into the faith and wishing to become a member and to an older one who has long been influenced by the life of the Christian community.

Every minister or leader conducting such a class must decide for himself how much time to devote to the elements involved, and how closely to tie his material to that in this Manual. He may well decide to present a copy to every member of the class at the very beginning. He may also find that many minor matters have been omitted and will want to incorporate them. Many concerns which are reckoned to be traditionally Methodist are not conspicuous here because the emphasis is on the training of contemporary Christians. Their need for an introduction to the Methodist heritage is an important but secondary one.

Bible references are to the *New English Bible*, but it is

suggested that Old Testament references should be found in the Revised Standard Version. It is useful for the members of a class to look up the references, which have been chosen in such a way as to help forward a discovery of the major books and themes of the Bible.

Normally a course in membership will conclude with a careful study of the service for the Public Reception of New Members (or 'Confirmation') and, perhaps at that point, the structure of the Communion Service. These are best studied by reference to the Book of Offices itself, so little mention is made of them here.

1. Becoming and Being a Christian

THERE is no standard way of becoming a Christian, for God in his goodness has made each of us distinctly different. Every individual is unique. There are as many ways of becoming a Christian as there are people. In Christianity nobody's experience is necessarily any better, any more reliable, any more valuable, than anyone else's. Every person who has become a Christian has travelled a marvellous and special road which no one else could tread in quite the same way. So we begin with a shout of praise to God who made each of us into distinct individuals, who guided and helped us in special ways that only we ourselves can know, and who brought us to the point of wanting to be pledged to Him and His Church.

If we were to take a close look at the roads along which many groups of Christians have come in their lives, we would probably find a collection of stories something like the following. Here, for example, is Eric who is now 20 and had never been in a Church until two years ago. He had left school and was well launched on his apprenticeship when he became acutely aware of the pettiness of his life, and found himself longing to do something more useful with it than merely to earn a living, enjoy a few luxuries at home and sample a few pleasures outside with his friends. He came into the Youth Club because he wanted to be doing things that would make the world a better place, and was drawn immediately into the Church's life and worship and faith. To his own surprise, he has found himself entering fully into the Christian life. It was exactly what he had been seeking, although he never knew it at the time.

She lived for kicks

Margaret was brought up to go to Sunday School with scrupulous regularity, but at 14 she suddenly decided she was having no more of it and left. Her parents didn't mind. She led a gay life and sampled every experience she could get. Sometimes she felt deeply ashamed of herself, but brushed those moments aside and lived for more kicks. One night a friend took her to an evangelistic service. It was just as if God spoke straight to her. She really wanted to be rid of the past and make a new start, so she answered the 'invitation' and was directed back to the Church she had deserted before. She had a tremendous enthusiasm for Christ and her work as a nurse has been transformed.

As good as gold

She is puzzled by Sylvia, who was in the same Sunday School class. Sylvia can never remember a time when she was not conscious of God, was not trying to serve Him, was not thoroughly involved in all the life of the Church. She comes from a devout Christian home and has always wanted to grow up in the faith by which her parents live. She wants to become a member of the Church because it is obviously the next stage in her own growing obedience to Christ.

To be really free

Her elder brother, Les, is quite different again. When he went off to University he was glad to clear out of the Church and get away from it all. He had two years of glorious freedom, during which he scandalised his family by the withering criticism he directed at the Church and by going to the local pub on Sunday evenings. Then in his third student year something began to change him, subtly but surely. He kept talking about 'realising my true self' and being 'accepted for what I am', whilst secretly he was more and more intrigued by the life and work of Jesus. Jesus seemed to him to be the only free, poised, balanced person who had ever lived. When he graduated and returned home to live and work he came one night to the communion service and announced afterwards that he must now become a member of the Church. He sums up his philosophy of life very simply by saying that he wants 'to be like Jesus'.

Real friendship

Yet all of them seem very immature to Mary Brown, now in her fifties and very quiet and shy. She has led a very ordinary life, marrying young and raising a son, looking after her little home and keeping herself carefully to herself and her family. But just after her son married and moved away, her husband was killed in a car crash, and Mary's life collapsed in ruins. She had to go out to work for the first time in her life, and always she was on her own. It was her neighbour who kept her life together by popping in during the evening, taking her out on Saturdays, introducing her to a fresh circle of friends, inviting her to Church. She wants to be a member because the Church is the one community now which really seems to care and to matter. She has found that at the heart of its life is a love for Jesus Christ which she is only too glad to give.

Moment of truth

Bill and Janet Spencer look at things differently again. They have three young children and can never forget a 'moment of truth' in their family life when the eldest child asked them one day, 'Why don't you teach us to pray? They teach us at school'. They couldn't answer, but next Sunday they took the children to Sunday School because Bill decided that he didn't want them to grow up like him, without any real faith at all. It wasn't long before they both realised that this wasn't quite good enough and they came to Church to learn what it was all about and whether it could indeed give their children a faith to live by. Within two years they found that they themselves were discovering just such a faith, that their whole pattern of living and conversation and family activity was being transformed. They now want to give a real lead to their children and to demonstrate purposeful lives, and have discovered that to be a Christian is the one clear way to do it.

'Many-splendoured thing'

And so we could go on. Take any group of Christian people at random, ask them the history of their lives, and this many-coloured picture results. It is there in the New Testament, of course. Paul became a Christian after years of struggling dissatisfaction as a believer in another religion altogether (the Jewish faith).[1] James became a Christian because he was Jesus' brother, growing up in the same home, and after the resurrection he became utterly convinced that Jesus had indeed been God's special agent in the world.[2] Matthew became a Christian after many dirty, shameful years cheating his fellows at the tax booth and the sudden chance to start a fresh, clean life.[3] The jailer at Philippi became a Christian after meeting the incredible courage of Christian prisoners who could have escaped but chose not to, thereby saving his life.[4] The Chancellor of the Ethiopian Exchequer became a Christian when someone could explain to him the whole purpose of God working right through history, foreseen in the Jewish prophets and made plain in Jesus Christ.[5]

Because there are so many different motifs in these stories the New Testament has a rich variety of descriptions for the Christian life. It is like being born all over again.[6] It is like being a superbly equipped Roman soldier, but for battle with evil.[7] It is like being a slave who is suddenly given his freedom, the ransom price having been paid by somebody else.[8] It is like standing in the court, guilty of a host of crimes, and hearing the judge send you out forgiven.[9] It is like being part of a triumphant army marching behind its general and receiving all sorts of good things from the spoils of war.[10] It is like being a poor slave who is taken into a loving family and adopted as a son.[11] It is like someone buying the greatest pearl in the world,[12] yet it is also like an athlete running in the Olympic games, watched by thousands.[13]

One Lord

Yet despite all these various motifs, pictures and life-stories there is one central experience which all indicate, describe or share, which is the key to the Christian's whole being. The Christian is a person for whom Jesus Christ matters more than anyone else, who loves Him with the deepest passion, who wants to obey Him and reproduce His virtues, who wants his life spent in the sort of service which Jesus offers the world and the sort of praise and obedience which Jesus offers to God the Father. The New Testament sums it up in one crisp phrase. The Christian is the one for whom Jesus is 'Lord'.[14]

This means that we cannot become Christians by chance, but only because we have opened up our lives to the purpose God first has for them. It means that we cannot drift into the Christian life unwittingly, like motoring from one county into another without realising it. To place one's life under Jesus' command requires a definite conscious pledge from us. It means that although it may have been a very costly and hard road, the result is inevitably an experience of release, discovery, freedom and joy.

Committed

And so there is now one thing that unites Eric, Margaret, Sylvia and Les, Mary Brown, Bill and Janet Spencer. They have been drawn into the Church through many different forces playing upon their lives but they have all come suddenly or slowly to the point at which they say, 'For me, from now on, Jesus is Lord'. They may still have a host of doubts about Christian doctrine, they may have all sorts of personal weaknesses which they haven't yet mastered and personal problems still to resolve, they may have had few 'spiritual experiences' when God seemed specially real and vivid to them, they may be in great confusion about what the Church stands for and highly critical of many of the things she does. But they are committed Christians because they have lined up their lives with Him and caught the first taste of His love.

Now they want to grow 'in Christ' and to express that pledge to Him throughout their lives.

References

1. See Acts 9, 1-19 or Romans 7.
2. 1 Corinthians 15,7.
3. Matthew 9,9.
4. Acts 16,19-34.
5. Acts 8,26-38.
6. John 3,1-8.
7. Ephesians 6,13-18.
8. 1 Peter 1,18,19. The techni-
cal term for the process is 'redemption'.
9. Romans 5,16.
10. Ephesians 4,8.
11. Galatians 4,7.
12. Matthew 13,46.
13. Hebrews 12,1.
14. Acts 2,36; 1 Corinthians 12,3.

There are many books which describe Christian people's spiritual pilgrimages. Of particular interest are Monica Furlong's *With Love to the Church* (in which she hints at her coming into faith via a broken marriage and much tenderness from a priest, and yet she is violently critical of the Church) or C. S. Lewis's *Surprised by Joy* (Fontana, in which he describes the very odd way in which he came into Christian certainty), or John Wesley's *Journal* (as abridged by Nehemiah Curnock: Epworth Press).

2. The Lordship of Christ

THE perpetual effort of Christian people to work out their allegiance to Christ in every aspect of their lives results in a quite distinctive pattern of living and behaviour, which we must now study carefully. We call this study 'Christian ethics', because ethics is the study of right and wrong behaviour. By the simple process of trying to be Christians at all we are involved in practising Christian ethics, so this is no academic concern.

The harsh hypocrites

A quick look at the New Testament shows that Christian ethics were clearly different from those of most Jews in Jesus' time. They sought to solve all problems of behaviour by setting out rules to be kept in every conceivable circumstance. The scribes were the experts in this process. The rules they devised to govern behaviour on the Sabbath, for instance, were notorious for their complexity. Jesus inevitably broke them because His life was inspired by a different spirit. He found that the keeping of them made people into harsh, censorious hypocrites who had lost their hold on the supreme virtue of love; he found that the whole system made people look to God as the Great Lawgiver, instead of the Father; He found that there was no help and encouragement for the weak and needy. So he was soon in basic conflict with many of his fellow-Jews, a conflict that lead ultimately to the Cross. Christian ethics, then, cannot be a matter of keeping a long list of rules and regulations.

Rules and regulations

Yet despite the plain evidence of the New Testament, there has always been the temptation in Christian circles to try to turn Christian behaviour into obedience to a code of rules. Sometimes there has been fairly good reason for this. It makes life simpler. It saves people from having to make up their own minds on difficult matters. It has helped in the maintenance of discipline within the Church and made it easier for Christians to prove to their governments that they are a law-abiding company. Most of us know how easy it has been within our own Church's life over the last hundred years to emphasise certain rules as if they were part and parcel of Christian behaviour, to be obeyed by all Christians in all circumstances (e.g. you must not gamble, you must not drink, etc.). Those rules were formulated as a result of grievous social problems and the urgent need for Christians to set a clear and wholesome example. But they are questioned deeply today because that attitude towards Christian behaviour cannot be reconciled with the spirit pervading the New Testament.

Teaching love

Jesus invites all men to live in 'the kingdom of God', to put our lives under God's complete control and direction. His earthly life showed what that was like, and his teaching explained it. He showed that to put one's life under God's control meant living so that love for God and man was the paramount motif, the vital determining factor. His teaching was a constant explanation of this, with the persistent challenge to his listeners to go and put it into practice. Thus he told the parable of the Good Samaritan both to explain what he meant by 'neighbour' (any person you encounter who is in need of your immediate help) and to make his questioner recognise it for himself and go and do likewise.[15] He taught us to see the supreme importance of every living creature and person because God does, so that this is a necessity for us if we are to take His love into our own lives.[16] He taught the necessity of forgiveness because God

14

is always forgiving and it is therefore an inevitable element in the whole practice of love.[17] He called for an indiscriminate concern for all people, good and bad alike, because God has, so His people must be finding value in all types of men and trying to love them.[18] He emphasised the showing of love towards flagrant sinners[19] and even enemies, because although we are most tempted to find excuses for avoiding such costly and risky loving, God does not shun the cost and risk (the willing death of Jesus being the supreme demonstration of this).[20]

Jesus, therefore, summed up Christian ethics by stating the two overriding concerns which must dominate the Christian man—'Love the Lord your God with all your heart, with all your soul, with all your mind and with all your strength' and 'Love your neighbour as yourself'.[21] St Paul wrote 'the whole law is summed up in love'[22] (and here he means by 'law' the will of God for our lives). St John wrote 'this is his command; to give our allegiance to His Son Jesus Christ and love one another as he commanded. When we keep his commands we dwell in him and he dwells in us'.[23] St Augustine, 300 years later, summed up the nature of Christian living in one daring sentence—'love and do what you will'.

With the grain

There is nothing naïve about this. Jesus was under no illusions about the dirty, mixed-up world in which we live. This is no starry-eyed idealism. His teaching was constantly reminding his listeners of the dangers, frustrations, costliness and hardship of this way of life.[24] Underlying it was Jesus' conviction that this universe was designed to express love and respond to it, so that the life of love is one that goes with the grain of all creation, that puts one into the *real* 'swim' of things, and sets one in basic harmony with the plan underlying all existence.

This supreme command to practise the life of love naturally means that there are very many things which the Christian will not do and will oppose with all his might.

15

Selfishness, snobbery, self-righteousness, self-importance are incompatible with love. The Christian sets his life firmly against them. He cannot be a person who harbours grudges, who ignores other people's needs, who is indifferent to suffering. He cannot be a party to anything which degrades human personality, since love perpetually works to exalt the human person. Hence he aims in a different direction from dissipation, or the cheapening of sex, or the mere hankering after one superficial pleasure after another. He knows that when love is at work in a community it results in fair play all round and in justice for all, so he is inevitably resisting injustice wherever it appears in the common life. To be directed by love means to turn one's back upon all forms of pettiness and selfishness, retaliation and hate.

Guidelines

Nor is the way of love necessarily vague, so that no general guidelines can be suggested which will normally characterise Christian conduct. As the last paragraph suggests, there are clearly some things which the Christian will not do, but others which he will do because they are almost always the way in which love will express itself. The ethical directions in the New Testament are of this nature. They are not absolute laws to be obeyed blindly whatever the circumstances, but guidelines which are normally right. So it is written 'Children, obey your parents in everything, for that is pleasing to God and is the Christian way,'[25] but clearly no child should obey a parent who commands him to steal from the old lady next door, or who wants to lead him away from the faith. Again, 'Every person must submit to the supreme authorities. There is no authority but by act of God',[26] but there are circumstances in which the government can become evil and might even have to be defied, as we notice later in the Bible where the Roman Government is referred to as 'the beast' and 'the great whore'.[27]

Times change

There are also many instances in which the ethical direc-

16

tions in the New Testament were valid outworkings of the law of love in that particular period and society, but cannot be held to be so for all eternity. Thus Paul required all women to cover their hair when in Church,[28] and elsewhere we are told that women must not become teachers.[29] Slaves were bidden to be submissive to their masters.[30] A man who would not work was to go without food.[31] Paul thought it preferable for people not to marry unless they could not contain themselves (but made a point of saying that it was his personal opinion and was not to be taken as a sure word from God—and he thought the world was coming to a speedy end!),[32] and for some Christians to go without meat because it came from the local temple and might scandalise anyone still very weak in the faith.[33]

What guidelines should apply to us today as we try to work out the basic drive of love for God and neighbour? Let us consider four aspects of our lives as contemporary Christians and attempt to outline the way in which the primacy of love may lead to certain specific commitments, attitudes and actions.

a. IN COMMUNITY AND WORLD AFFAIRS

The Christian is automatically committed to love the world's life by throwing himself unreservedly into the whole struggle to meet men's needs, to obtain good government, to root out injustice and inhumanity wherever they occur, to serve his fellow men. He is committed to the world in this way because Christ was and is, because God so loves the world that He is perpetually pouring His mercy and justice into it in order to promote real life for all men. But there is a sense in which the Christian must *not* love the world—he must not admire the world's stunted sense of values, its constant hankering after little gods of its own devising, its incessant attempt to try to find satisfaction in small, selfish living. The Christian must not love the world's refusal to take God seriously, its attempts to avoid God, to run away from God, to ignore God.

Many Christians have wrongly concluded that the New

Testament takes such a jaundiced view of the world's life that we must try to disentangle ourselves from it as much as possible. This makes it vitally important that we see clearly the distinction made above. When John writes, 'Anyone who loves the world is a stranger to the Father's love,'[34] he is referring to a false admiration for the way the world tries to live without obeying God at all. Paul gives similar advice when he writes, 'Adapt yourselves no longer to the pattern of this present world, but let your minds be remade'.[35] For the Christian, his whole cast of mind, the direction in which he wants his life to go, the things for which he wishes to live, are determined by the God who has shown himself in Christ. They are not determined by the easy-going self-centredness of the world's style of life. The Christian turns his back on that whole attitude so that he can really love and serve mankind's needs alongside Jesus Christ. He loves mankind and the purposes God has put into all creation—so in *that* sense he loves the world. It is in *that* sense that God loves the world and gives His Son to it.[36]

Yes to Politics

Therefore the Christian is bound to be a person who is deeply concerned about the crucial social issues of our day, who is bound to get caught up in the struggle for righteousness on all sides. He is automatically a person who is concerned about politics, about fair wages and good Trade Unionism, about a local Council that is alert to cater for the genuine needs of the neighbourhood without pandering to any vested interests and pressure groups, about an accurate press and an honest police force, about just laws and good welfare facilities, about decent housing conditions and good planning, about enlightened schooling and clean streets. He is automatically a person who may not sit back in his armchair and leave all those problems to other people (on the spurious grounds that 'politics is a dirty business'). They are the problems of how to organize the human family decently, the problems involved in loving one's neighbour.

Ten Bob a Week!

Within this political concern there are three key issues at present which need to be spotlighted. The first is world hunger and poverty. It matters profoundly to the Christian that the 470 million people of India have an average weekly income of under 10s. per week, whilst the 340 million of Western Europe have £7 per week, and the tendency is for that gap to get bigger, not less. It gets bigger because the over-riding concern of Western European governments is to increase the standard of living of *their* people. Whereas most people could not care less, the Christian knows that those people are real people of flesh and blood, not merely colourless statistics, and that Christ died for them and now lives for them. The Christian can never forget Jesus' words, 'When I was hungry you gave me nothing to eat'.[37]

Christ is Colour Blind

The second is race. All over the world the coloured man is demanding to be treated with a new dignity, but all over the world the white man fears him and has a peculiar sense of uneasiness towards him. Influential voices are raised suggesting that multiracial living is impossible because the races have been made so distinctly different and because the lighter-skinned ones have certain superiorities. The Christian knows that those voices are wrong, tragically wrong. God made all men of one stock[38] to live together as one family of equals, whilst Christ died as the central act of God in pulling all mankind together and setting us rightly under His rule.[39] Therefore he is bound to work for harmony between all races, he is bound to abhor a colour bar, bound to feel shame that a Race Relations Act has been found necessary in Britain.

Ban the Bomb!

The third issue is war. It is always contrary to the mind of Jesus Christ, but modern nuclear war becomes worse and is tantamount to blasphemy (the denial that God has made other nations so that they have a right to exist). To threaten nuclear war is such an integral part of our nation's policy that few Christians realise the moral problem we live with. The Christian must be under no illusions about it, especially when 'defence' requires so much of the nation's energy and resources. Whilst some Christians believe it to be the lesser of two evils to support the modern war machine and the policies that go with it, others are bound to query whether a person committed to Christ's way of love can actively support the machine or its policies or could ever serve in the armed forces, or work in the armament factories. Meanwhile all Christians are obliged to work for an effective U N O to serve the world as an agency for understanding, peace and international co-operation.

b. IN DEALING WITH OTHER PEOPLE

People matter. All people are made by God with the intention that they may know themselves to be His children and live accordingly.[40] All people have the unspeakable privilege of the offer of God's love, the wonder of Christ having died for them and now being alive for them. That is true of every person whether he knows it or not—rich or poor, dirty or clean, ignorant or well-educated, nice or nasty, young or old, crude or genteel, weak or strong. To the Christian, everyone of them is a unique exampe of the creative range of God's love. To the Christian, Christ is Lord over them all.

This transforms the way the Christian behaves towards others, whether in the bus, or at work, or in the street, or over the garden fence, or in the shop or on the beach or on the roads. In particular, it transforms his attitude towards family life and the tremendous power of sex whereby God binds man and woman together and continues the human race.

Bless this house

Consider family life first. Each member of the family is of equal importance to God, the parents being appointed by Him to exercise leadership and to set the tone of the family's loving. Within the Christian family there is, therefore, the God-given opportunity to discover that mutual respect between young and old which is essential for the happiness of both and the general well-being of the whole community.[41] At present the need for genuine understanding between the age groups is deeply important—the Christian family being the key place within which it can be discovered. The home in which the mother is treated as a slave by the father or the children; in which the father's task is simply to earn the housekeeping money; in which the children are regarded as a nuisance or as cheap and easy labour or are there to be seen and not heard; in which any age group is ostracised or outraged by any other; in which the aged and infirm are of no account; or to which the teenager will contribute nothing but appearances to eat and sleep; is that travesty from which Christ continually works to deliver us, because it expresses no respect for persons. That home which is merely a petty little citadel in which a few people hide their mutual selfishness; from which no goodwill ever emanates outside; into which no visitor is ever welcomed; through which no larger needs are ever met; is likewise a travesty from which Christ works to deliver us, for it expresses no concern for the world. The Christian family has the God-given chance to escape such perversions. It is intended to be the place within which each person's worth is respected and not exploited, but contributed freely to the common good.

Sex is to be enjoyed

Now let us consider sex. The modern world, as we all know, is fascinated by sex to such a degree that a cool appreciation of this uniquely creative gift of God is rare indeed. But there is a straightforward appreciation of it in the Bible which sometimes sounds almost crude, as when Paul tells the married not to abstain from sexual intercourse for very long, or they put their marriage under great strain,[42] or when it includes a frank love song in which the two lovers sing the praises of each others' bodies.[43] The latter passage is a perpetual reminder to us that there is no prudery whatever in the Christian's approach to sex—he starts by seeing

21

it realistically, by seeing it as a gift of God which we are meant to *enjoy*, but which we can only enjoy fully when we appreciate what the gift is for.

Adam needs Eve and she needs Adam

The Bible makes it plain that there are three main purposes within the gift of sex, all of them linked with the purposes of love running through all creation. God has created the two distinct sexes so as to make life far more interesting all round. It is a dull world without two sexes, suggested by the picture of Adam being miserably lonely, and uninspired until Eve stood at his side.[44] The first purpose of sex, then, is to make all human community far more lively and stimulating. It means that there are always two contrasting human responses in every situation—the male and the female—the contrast being good for us because it makes life much more fascinating.

One flesh

Secondly, sex is the gift whereby two persons are able to enter into a total commitment to each other, to experience something of the fulness, the heights and lengths and breadths and depths of love. Through marriage a man and woman are enabled to interlock their interests, their prayers, their deepest desires, their whole practice of living, their bodies, their whole beings. But it is the strength within sex which really cements this whole union and gives to it a magnetic gripping power. The resulting union is termed 'one flesh' in the Bible.[45] In it, both personalities become immeasurably enriched and developed, since loving and being loved in this total way is one of the most salutary experiences the human personality can have. It is one of the clearest reproductions we can experience of the total love of God for us—hence the quite astounding claim which Paul makes, that the love between husband and wife is like that between Christ and His Church.[46]

Thirdly, sex is the gift whereby human beings can share with God His joy in creation. To be able to have children,

22

to rear them and tend them, is intended by God to give us an inkling of this special joy which lies at the heart of all creation. So husband and wife share together in the creative grace of God which is what makes life, what makes each separate child into a distinct, unrepeatable person.[47]

Handling sex

It is with this understanding of the role of sex that the Christian tries to resolve all the subtle moral issues which sex raises. Sex is not, to him, 'dirty' and therefore is not the subject of dirty jokes or obscenity. It is not primarily a gift to enable us to have pleasure, or bodily satisfaction, so he shuns every sort of behaviour which merely aims at getting easy thrills from it. Always that approach tends to cheapen people, to reduce them to mere thrill-producers and in the extreme (such as in prostitution) almost reduces them to the level of the beasts. The man or woman who is only able to view the opposite sex as a source of sexual pleasure is one who has already degraded human persons (and, in the process, degraded himself).

Again, the Christian sees sexual intercourse as an act of peculiar power with a profound meaning, which needs an appropriate setting to convey it fully. Christians believe that marriage is this setting. Only within marriage are two partners really able to tell each other that they are totally committed to each other (since they have only become so committed through marriage). Whenever that act occurs outside marriage it falls short of what God intended, and frequently produces distress and damage to people and their lives. It is also obvious from this that marriage is only valid when this full meaning of total commitment holds good. *Nobody* should marry unless it does, whatever pressures are upon him or her.

Divorce?

This Christian understanding of the significance of sex is also a guide to the frequently-debated issues of birth control and divorce. It is because sex is not merely a gift to enable human beings to reproduce the species but has a much fuller purpose within marriage, that the Methodist Church sees a distinctly valuable function for birth control. Within marriage it is not normally right to practice birth control to avoid having children altogether, but it is right to further a family pattern which has been planned (as far as that is possible). Again, if two persons' commitment to each other has tragically evaporated it may be right to cut the marriage tie, since that marriage has lost all its inner meaning. Hence there are circumstances in which it may be right to divorce a partner, and some circumstances in which it may be right to marry someone else.[48]

Marriage isn't for all

Despite the highly important role of sex within every life and the high view of marriage which Christian faith gives to us, it would nevertheless be wrong to imply that an unmarried person ought to be pitied. Jesus was unmarried—but was *wholly* a man. There are many people who are much more free to serve God if they do not have the major responsibility of looking after a partner and raising a family, and clearly Jesus was one.[49] There are many people who have no chance of being linked with a suitable partner and are better not to marry since an unhappy marriage is sheer hell. But, more positively, there are means of sublimating the energies of sex so that they become of the utmost value to the human community (most obviously in professions like nursing, teaching, etc.).

When a Christian marries, let him marry a Christian.[50] It should be the aim of every Christian to establish a Christian home, to share the same ideals and faith with the partner, to bring children up in the faith, to make the partnership part of a total service and offering to God and man. Therefore, if a Christian marries someone from another denomination it is necessary to decide which Church they can share in *together*. Those whom God has joined together, let not denominations put asunder . . . .

c. THE USE OF PERSONAL GIFTS

All Christians have to work out what the Lordship of Christ over their own personal abilities and possessions must mean. It is a costly and exacting exercise, which has to be repeated over and over again right through one's life. Consider money, to begin with. We shall be using money every day until we die, and every day we are inevitably deciding what is right to do with it by the normal processes of spending and saving. The particularly vicious power of money to dominate our lives is plainly announced in the Bible,[51] with the frequent warning that we be on our guard so that we master our money and not vice versa.[52]

Money is Power

What does it mean to master money? The Jews used to give a tenth of their income to God (called a tithe).[53] Paul taught his people to set aside a certain sum every Sunday, specifically for the needs of the Church and proportionate to their income.[54] This is obviously the first thing we should do—to set aside from our wages what is a right (and generous) sum. Many Christians today find that 5% (i.e. a shilling in every pound) of their 'take-home' pay is about the right amount. If our Church runs a Stewardship Scheme, this makes our giving very straightforward; if not, we can still keep that sum aside to cover all our Church giving.

But after that? There are two main requirements from our money. It must enable us to maintain our own lives and any others for whom we are responsible with self-respect and dignity, but not with indulgence, extravagance, or plain selfishness. It must also enable us to do good in the world, for money is a power that achieves enormous good when directed shrewdly. Many good things *cannot* be achieved without the power of money. But there are no laws here for the Christian—only the constant reminder from Christ that money is for human wellbeing, not for personal advantage,[55] and hence the constant need to see that we carry out a faithful stewardship with it. The Christian cannot be a mean man.

Jobs for all

The major problem which is inevitably linked with our use of money is, of course, the means by which we gain it and the type of work to which we commit our abilities. We believe that God has a distinct purpose for every life, and from this Christians derive their understanding of 'vocation' —that God will call us into the right life-work if we will let him and if we go about it in the right sort of way. It is just as likely that God will have a vocation for one person to be a scientist as for another to be a minister, for one person to be a housewife and mother whilst another is a nurse, for one to be an engineer and another an actor. Some of these tasks matter more urgently to the life of the Church than others (e.g. there is a critical shortage of ministers), some of them more directly involved with great human need (e.g. nursing), so that those vocations need to feature most clearly in the Church's concerns—but every Christian who has found his right niche in life must have first found God's vocation for him, whatever his job happens to be.

No voices in the night

The Christian's certainty about his vocation does not usually come about in weird ways—God does not speak to us with a loud voice when we are saying our prayers, nor does he normally direct us by odd 'signs' and freak happenings. He generally guides us through enlightened common-sense, the constant pressure of everyday events, and consultation with other Christians who understand the problem. If we have been given certain obvious aptitudes, our common-sense tells us that we should use them fully. Thus a person with a deep love for the land is probably being guided by God through that deep love to become a farmer. If there is only one job we can take when we leave school, and we discover it is totally absorbing and rewarding to us, we accept that as God's guidance to us through those circumstances. If other Christians are sure that a certain job is utterly right for us this is most likely a word from God.

The Christian is, nevertheless, given special help by God

in simple ways. God gives him a sense of values which nobody else quite has, and these affect his whole response to every situation. Thus the Christian discovers that it is much more rewarding to him personally if he is using his talents so as to help mankind and meet human needs—God has built into him, as it were, a capacity to love being a useful servant of men, and a distaste for being an exploiter. The Christian has built into him a certain willingness to take good and healthy risks (knowing that he is ultimately upheld by God), whereas many people crave for a concrete security at all times. The Christian is given a special concern for people and human personality, so that he can only find real peace in work which has a certain human warmth within it. But beyond that, God also influences him through crucial needs. Where there are gaps (e.g. the present shortage of teachers, or ministers or prison warders), this is to the Christian a special urgent pressure from God upon him.

Ambitious?

A vocation, then, is a certainty about one's life work which has come about by being specially alert to the pressures of God upon one, through the obvious facts of one's situation, through certain great gaps which one has become aware of, through the scale of values by which the Christian judges life. A Christian may well be a dustman or a director, to mention two of many openings, but there are certain sorts of work he can hardly ever do; he cannot make shoddy goods that are a swindle, nor can he sell them. He cannot be involved in foisting something harmful on to people (e.g. the drug traffic. Selling spirits?). He can hardly be involved in trivial occupations, in perpetrating lies, in wasting his own abilities or those of others. But it is quite legitimate that he should have ambitions as long as his overriding one is to be obedient to Christ his Lord.

d. THE PRACTICE OF PERSONAL DEVOTION

The personal devotions of a Christian are an essential part of his constant intention to show an all-out obedience to

Jesus Christ as Lord, to serve God and man with the spontaneous freedom which Jesus demonstrated, to live 'in the kingdom'. It is necessary to say this at the very beginning because many people regard prayer as a means of getting some sort of favour from God, a means of altering things to suit themselves, a type of magic whereby supernatural powers can be called in on their side for what they want. This is not Christian prayer, it is more like primitive paganism. Christian prayer is the conscious offering of one's life to God in Christ, the opening of one's whole being to His wishes and strength, the speaking of our deepest desires to Him so that He can change them where necessary. One does not aim to get God to help us achieve what *we* want, one aims to be placed at His disposal to achieve what *He* wants.

Prayers can be short

When we know precisely what we are doing when we pray, then there are no rules and regulations about it whatever. Each person must sort out his own practice to be appropriate to his pattern of life. For some people, the best time to give an uninterrupted time to God may be early in the morning, for others it may be last thing at night, for a housewife it may be after breakfast when the family has just left for work and school. Nor is it necessarily more valuable for us to spend 20 minutes than 5 in prayer. What matters is the wholeheartedness with which we offer the time. (Note that the Lord's Prayer is extremely short and lasts about a minute.)

Whilst there are no laws, here are some guidelines. Be chary of spiritual heroics. Aim for a simple regular practice of devotion, and slowly build it up and develop it as you are able. Do not screw yourself up into huge promises to spend an hour a day praying, as a result of which the whole exercise becomes a massive duty, heavy and burdensome.

Antidote to idolatry

Build into your devotions a regular practice of Bible reading. There is one elementary reason for this. The God to whom we look and to whom we offer our lives is the God and Father of our Lord, Jesus Christ. He has shown us what he is like through the Bible. If we soak our minds in the Bible, we are soaking our minds in the valid news about the real God—whereas otherwise we end up having a belief in 'God' which is a make-believe of our own concoction (what the Bible denounces as an 'idol'). There are various schemes of Bible reading which can help us here, about which we should obtain advice—but at all costs, do not indulge in the rather futile exercise of reading a chapter of the Bible each day from cover to cover beginning in Genesis, or you will very soon be profoundly bored. The Bible is *not* to be read like that. It is a library and we need simple guidance about tackling it.

Borrow God's eyes

Within the Christian's devotions, then, there will be attention to the Bible. There will obviously be a great deal of sheer thanksgiving and delight in the goodness of God. There will be confession of failure and blindness and weakness (make it honest. It is vain for us to belittle our sins, and equally vain for us to exaggerate them). There will be an offering of the time ahead. There will be prayer for others, for the world, for the Church, for the whole host of people and things which the Christian finds himself being concerned about. The aim for these intercessory prayers will be for us to share rightly in the concern which God already has for them, almost as if we 'borrow God's eyes' to look at that little part of the world in which He has put us. There will be a plea for the help of the Holy Spirit, for us to have the mind which was in Christ so that we can behave like Him.

We do not have to cultivate a special 'religious' way of speaking. God has no particular preference for the language of the Authorised Version of the Bible. He simply wants us to be ourselves in the freest way possible, so we talk with Him as we would with Jesus Christ if He was present in the flesh just beside us. Sometimes, to be sure, we find ourselves strangely tongue-tied. We don't know what to say.

Then we can do either of two things. We needn't say anything. Instead, we can try to *imagine* Jesus Christ active here (or, if it is easier, imagine Him in Palestine in the way the gospels describe). Alternatively, we can use other people's prayers from a book. They can often be a superb help to get us going, whilst the choicest prayers (like some of the Psalms) are a permanent boon to those who have committed them to memory.

God seems dead

Because we are human the very best of us is liable to get times of spiritual dryness and despair, times when God seems a long way off and prayer seems unreal, times when we wonder whether the whole thing is not a big make-believe, times when we long for the enthusiasm and joy which we once had but which seems to have deserted us, times when we frankly do not 'feel like it'. This experience may come to us because we have let God down and secretly we know it. We may have had a deep quarrel with somebody very important to us, we may have failed miserably with a responsibility given to us (perhaps by the Church) or we may have indulged some basic weakness in ourselves. The way through this problem is to come clean to God and then to man, to tell God the whole issue and then, in His new peace, to set about trying to put it right. We shall never gain peace by running away, like Jonah.

No baby

But this spiritual depression may not be due to our personal failures. It may be something which has happened to us for no apparent reason. In which case, do not despair! We are so made that most of us cannot go on for ever in the same emotional condition; our natures require certain ups and downs. This is not a bad thing, any more than it is bad for tides to regularly come in and out, thereby keeping the beach fresh and clean. Accept this as part of our make-up. When we get into a dull patch let us maintain our trust in God by the simple process of continuing to talk honestly to

Him, telling Him how tired we are, how remote He seems, how difficult it is to pray, how boring we find the Church service, how fed up we are with ourselves. He keeps faith with us, and the dull times have a strange way of turning us into stronger, wiser Christians who have grown out of spiritual babyhood into maturity. Most youngsters experience growing pains, after all.

There is also need for us to develop the simple art of contemplation: the ability to sit quietly and focus our attention on some truth of God and His work, turning it over and over in our mind without rush, and checking the tendency for our thought to flit away on to something else. Again, a book will often help us to get going, while the print on the page before us helps us to keep our mind from wandering.

References

15. Luke 10,29-37.
16. Matthew 10,29-30.
17. Matthew 18,23-35.
18. Matthew 5,44,45.
19. Luke 19,1-10; John 8,2-11.
20. Romans 5,6-8.
21. Mark 12,28-31.
22. Romans 13,10.
23. 1 John 3,23.
24. Mark 8,34;13,9-13.
25. Colossians 3,20.
26. Romans 13,1 or 1 Peter 2, 13-15.
27. Revelation 13,1 and 17,1.
28. 1 Corinthians 11,5.
29. 1 Timothy 2,12.
30. 1 Peter 2,18; 1 Timothy 6,1.
31. 2 Thessalonians 3,10.
32. 1 Corinthians 7,25-40.
33. 1 Corinthians 8.
34. See the passage 1 John 2, 15-17.
35. Romans 12,2.
36. John 3,16.
37. See the passage Matthew 25, 31-46.
38. Acts 17,26.
39. Galatians 3,28; Revelation 7,9,10.
40. 1 Timothy 2,4-6.
41. Ephesians 6,1-4; 1 Thessalonians 2,10-12.
42. 1 Corinthians 7,5.
43. The Song of Songs.
44. Genesis 2,20.
45. Genesis 2,24; Mark 10,8.
46. Ephesians 5,21-33.
47. 1 Peter 3,7.
48. In Matthew 5,31 & 32, Jesus says that divorce is permissible in the case of adultery.
49. Matthew 19,12.
50. 2 Corinthians 6,14.
51. 1 Timothy 6,10; Luke 12, 13-21.
52. Matthew 6,24.
53. Leviticus 27,30-32.
54. 1 Corinthians 16,1,2.
55. Mark 10,17-27.

3. The Church

THE Church is the gift of God to every Christian whereby he is given the means to grow 'in Christ', the family of God which finds its existence in worshipping Him, the company through which Christ wishes to continue and fulfil all his work for mankind. The question whether or not one can be a Christian without 'going to Church' is a hypothetical one. What is certain is that nobody first becomes a Christian except through the constant influence of the Church and nobody can maintain a Christian life without being a member of the household of God. The Christian naturally shares in the life of that household because it is *only* there that Christ is worshipped and adored and the prime means of Christ's help are to be found.

There is a sense in which the Church has been built by men. Its buildings have obviously been erected by men, its teaching comes through men, its divisions are clearly due to men's differing reactions, and its company consists of human beings. But there is a more important sense in which the Church is not built by men. The first creation of the Church was by act of God in giving Jesus Christ to his world.[56] The belief of the Church, which alone gives it any usefulness, centres upon what God has done.[57] The news which the Church is to proclaim is news about God and His deeds in Christ.[58] The tasks of the Church are those which we first see in Jesus Christ and know Him to be doing now with all the everlasting energy of God.[59]

To be a Christian is to be caught up in all this activity, all this purpose, this worship, this energy. To be a Christian is to open one's life up to what God has done and is doing through Jesus Christ, so it inevitably means sharing in the ongoing life of His Church.

a. THE WORSHIP OF THE CHURCH

The main point of worship is not to make us feel better, to listen to brilliant orations, to be stirred up by mighty singing, to be with a good crowd, to be fascinated by the mysterious power of the sacraments, or to get away from the worries of normal existence. The supreme point is that we worship God. We do this by celebrating the gospel, by rejoicing in what He has done for us and our world, and what He continues to do and ever will do.[60] A 'good' service is one in which this celebration is clear, sincere, wholehearted—whatever the preacher, the hymns, the atmosphere at communion, the size of the congregation, etc.

Some Celebration!

A by-product of the celebration is that it indeed makes us feel better, it builds us up and encourages us to live in Christ, it links us up with a special group of people, it puts new ideas into our minds and songs on to our lips, it enables us to face up to life with a fresh and healthy confidence. But these are by-products and we can only enjoy worship properly when we do not seek these things first, but simply try to rejoice in God and the good news about Him which Christ embodies.

Three simple features are normally involved in Christian worship—our approach to God and awareness that we are in His presence, our listening to the message which he has for us, and our glad response to this gospel by offering ourselves to live by its truth and in Christ. The opening part of worship is meant to express that first feature (and will include praise, confession of our sins, thanksgiving), the readings and sermon to express the second, the sacrament of holy communion, prayers for the world, and dedication of ourselves to express the third.

Symbol and Sacrament

The sacraments require special appreciation from us. There are two—Baptism and Communion. The latter is called by many different terms by the different churches—e.g. the Eucharist, the Last Supper, the Lord's Supper, the Breaking of Bread, the Mass. A sacrament is a special means chosen by Christ for proclaiming the gospel, using symbols (water in baptism, bread and wine in communion). It is clear that Jesus commanded His people to practice these two sacraments as a regular feature of the life of His people.[61] But both sacraments have been grievously misunderstood and there is still widespread confusion about their meaning and importance.

Baptism is the simple symbolic act in which Christ declares that He has died and now lives for that particular person so that all His promises of new life hold good, and in which He brings him into the company of His people, the Church, through the present work of the Holy Spirit. When an adult person is baptised this is linked with his formal reception into the full membership of the Church and therefore a further declaration is being made—a declaration that he or she knows Christ to have done this, accepts the promises of Christ and has entered into the new life, pledged to be a faithful member of the Church.

Because most of those being baptised in New Testament times were adults who had not first been brought up in Christian homes, their baptisms had this full declaration, both that which Christ makes in the actual act and that which a believer can make in response. Accordingly, the New Testament teaches the profound importance of baptism.[62] It stresses that the Holy Spirit is at work.[63] To put it in another way, the living power of Christ is clearly operative here.

Baby Baptism?

But from very early times children and babies were baptised, and there are hints of this practice even in the New Testament.[64] When a new-born baby is baptised, Christ is making the same declarations even though the person con-

34

cerned cannot yet make any response. The baby is becoming a 'baby member' of the Church's family. Later when that child has grown up and has determined to live for Christ, the act will have its completion (or 'confirmation') in the reception of that person into full membership and then that believer will make his own declaration of faith and discipleship.

The Methodist Church practises infant baptism. If someone wishes to became a member and has not first been baptised, an adult baptism will be included within the Reception into Full Membership (or Confirmation). It is not right that we should become members of the Church without ever having been baptised, since from the very beginning this has been an essential sign of our reception by God into His family.[65] It is pointless for a person to want to be baptised twice. Once Christ's appointed act of declaration has been done for a person, it must hold good for ever or it is pointless anyway.

Nobody is 'good enough'

The sacrament of Holy Communion is commonly misunderstood in two ways. Many people regard it as special act of dedication which only the very saintly can make, so they avoid it by saying, 'I'm not good enough'. Others suspect that it involves some strange magical process which they cannot quite believe and which savours of hocus pocus. Let us begin with the act of Jesus. During the last meal which He shared with His friends He wished to institute an effective means whereby they could remember Him and His offering of his whole being for them and to God, and in which they could demonstrate their complete certainty that He was still with them, alive but unseen. The two basic elements of their meal were bread and wine, so He chose them as the symbols of His body and blood (i.e. His total giving of His life for us). The early Church immediately found in the 'breaking of bread' the key feature of its life together and its worship of the risen Jesus.[66]

It is obvious then, that Jesus did not intend this act to be one for the very saintly only, but for every person who wishes to remember Him, receive His help, and serve Him. One who feels especially unsatisfactory as a Christian is most especially invited to His table by Christ. Nor is there any magical process at work. We believe that the bread and wine act as tokens and pledges of Christ's love and self-giving for us—just as a wedding ring acts as a token and pledge of a husband's love for his wife. But because the nature of this service was first instituted by Jesus Himself, the Church has always believed that we should be especially careful so to practise the service that its full meaning will be preserved, which is why the Methodist Church normally takes great care to follow the service from its Book of Offices, as prescribed by the Church.

What happens?

When we take part in a communion service there are certain plain things that we are doing. We are putting ourselves along with Jesus' disciples without making any pretence about our worthiness (after all, Judas Iscariot was invited by Jesus to the original supper). We are giving thanks to God for His gift of His Son ('celebrating the gospel'), and we are rejoicing at the way Jesus himself was so obedient to God as to die for our sakes. We are being bound together as one people who all need and receive the same nourishment without distinction. We are putting our lives at His disposal and receiving the pledge of His help in as intimate a way as eating and drinking. We are remembering Jesus as He has invited us to do. We are marvelling at the way Jesus uses the ordinary things of the world (bread and wine) to represent Him, a marvel which helps us to look at the things of the world with fresh eyes altogether. And we are getting a glimpse of what heaven is like—heaven is to be in perfect harmony with God and His people, God alone being the powerhouse for everyone's existence, man's selfishness and sin having been obliterated.

It is understandable then, that the Methodist Church regards the two sacraments as being founded by Jesus and a perpetual obligation within the life of the Church. It regards them as especial 'means of grace', and expects its members to avail themselves of the privilege of the Lord's Supper gladly and constantly. When Jesus Christ invites, his friends rejoice, come, and receive.

b. THE CHRISTIAN FESTIVALS

The Christian 'year' begins with Advent, four Sundays before Christmas. On this Sunday and the ones that immediately follow, the Church looks forward to the coming of Christ, prepares for Christmas, and looks forward to His ultimate deed at the completion of all things.

At Christmas she celebrates the gift of Jesus Christ, the chosen agent or 'Son' of God, born in Bethlehem. Immediately afterwards she celebrates Epiphany, which features the way in which Jesus is worshipped by people from other countries (the wise men) and is shown to be sent for all the world. At about the same time the Methodist Church holds its Annual Covenant Service on the first Sunday of the New Year, so that its people may begin the year with a searching act of dedication first used by John Wesley and preserved to this day because of its spiritual value.

Easter to Whit

'Lent' is a 40-day period of preparation for Easter, beginning on Ash Wednesday (sometime in February or March). It is used by Christians to try to develop a real sorrow for their sins and to practise self-sacrifice. The Sunday coming two weeks before Easter is specifically devoted to the suffering of Christ (Passion Sunday), and the following one celebrates His riding into Jerusalem on a donkey to face the final ordeal there (Palm Sunday). That final week in Jesus' life is celebrated as 'Holy Week' and is used to give a particular appreciation of the meaning of His death. On the Thursday of Holy Week (Maundy Thursday) many Churches will hold a communion service because on that original Thursday evening the communion was first instituted.

'Good Friday' is the day upon which Jesus was crucified. It is called 'good' because Christians see in His behaviour then the final and most convincing evidence of His goodness and total willingness to give His everything to God and for men. On 'Easter Day' we rejoice in His resurrection, His victory over death and evil, His liberation to be with His people for ever. Forty days later comes the day when Jesus 'ascended into heaven' (Ascension Day is a Thursday), which signifies that his physical body was dispensed with and He was fully freed to be 'with God' and so be everywhere. Ten days later comes Whit Sunday, the day on which the powers of Jesus' now ascended life were first let loose amongst His friends. This is the gift of the Holy Spirit.

This day was originally called Pentecost amongst the Jews.

Three in One, and One in Three!

The following Sunday is called 'Trinity Sunday' because the whole sequence of the year up until then has been setting out the vital features of the Christian's faith in God—or, to put it in another way, it has been setting out how God has shown Himself to us. He has shown himself to us in three aspects of his being—as God the Father who has made all things and all persons, as Jesus Christ who is God revealed amongst us to save and help us, as the Holy Spirit who is the energy of Jesus alive and at work within us now.

After Trinity Sunday there follows a long period right through summer and autumn within which there is no specific festival, except that Christians usually choose a Sunday in the autumn to thank God for His continued provision for our need of food and the basic necessities of life, the Harvest Festival. This obviously lends itself to a celebration of God as Creator and Lord of all life.

c. THE CHURCH'S TASK ON EARTH

It is a sign of our blindness to the real task of the Church that we talk about 'Church work' as being a matter of raising money for it, or attending committees and meetings connected with its life. The first work of the Church is to worship God continuously, celebrating the gospel so that all may hear and rejoice in the good news. Along with this goes the continuous call of God to work for Him in the world or, to put it in another way, to share with Christ in the everlasting labour of love which He pours into the world's life.

Let us look more carefully at this task. If we were to ask what Jesus Christ is actually doing here and now, we would get the same answer as He Himself supplied right at the beginning of his earthly work when he explained his purposes. Jesus said then:

'He has sent me to announce good news to the poor,

To proclaim release for prisoners and recovery of
sight for the blind,

To let the broken victims go free,

To proclaim the year of the Lord's favour.'[67]

Not just talk

At first sight this seems to be mainly a matter of talking, of proclaiming, of preaching. But whenever the Bible mentions words and speech and proclamation it does not simply mean our exercising our tongues so as to make certain sounds with them, it means both speaking and at the same time *doing* the things about which we speak. This is made plain in Jesus' own life. He did not merely talk about these things, He proceeded to *do* them—He rejoiced the poor, He set people free from every sort of bondage, he healed the sick and the blind, He was astonishingly tender to the broken-down and down-trodden, He showed in every conceivable way that God was acting for every man's well-being here and now, that it was the year of the Lord's favour.

Up the down-and-outs

This gives us the necessary direction for the Church's task, which must be one of speech and of action. Is it fair to say that the Church has often preferred to do a lot of speaking, but has not always wanted to accompany it with action? If so, let us look first at the sort of action that is appropriate for the Church's task. Clearly the victims, the under-dogs, the under-privileged have a special place within her labours, she being the one body who will be most concerned for their welfare. So a major task of the Church is to care for them, whether they are young or old. From this conviction has sprung the Church's work amongst orphans, down-and-outs, unmarried mothers, drug addicts, tramps, alcoholics, the aged, and so on. From it has sprung the zeal of Christian men to found Trade Unions, abolish slavery, join the American negro freedom movement, etc.

The prisoners cannot be forgotten, that section of the community which society has decided to dispose of for the time being. Jesus works to bring them release, which surely means a return to normal decent living and the chance of a life of full health in Christ. It is not the Church's role to be working for punishment, but for every erring person's total reclamation. Blind people feature in Jesus' work, and with them all who are afflicted with any sort of sickness. So it becomes the Church's work to bring healing to all who are sick; hence the constant concern that Christians have ever had for hospitals, healing, nursing, the whole health of the whole man.

The Church looks out

In each age and situation this outgoing concern for humanity has to be adapted to meet the local conditions. If a Welfare State is able to take over some of these functions, thanks be to God. There will always be gaps in their provision, areas of fresh need not yet catered for, points at which Christians are needed to contribute a special human warmth and personal concern into what may otherwise be a formal piece of welfare machinery. The Church's concern for youth, for example, is bound to have an extra element to the concern shown by government bodies.

This means that the Church's task in every local situation becomes the dual one of proclamation and of setting about meeting the human needs round about. But we live in an age when this has been widely forgotten by most Churches. Because Church attendance has been declining all through this century the average Church expends almost all its energy on trying to keep going, trying to hold on to its people, trying to get as many as possible on to its premises, trying to preserve its own life. It becomes obsessed with its own self—and we are back with the picture we started with of Church work being a matter of raising money and going to meetings on the Church premises. A major task of the contemporary Christian is to direct his Church's concerns to the needs outside her walls and away from the internal problems. The basic spiritual law of Jesus that 'He who loses his life shall save it' applies precisely here.

The Church looks in

But are we not to bother with what goes on within the Church's life? Of course we are. It is important that the steady worshipping life of the Church is surrounded by her own training and teaching agencies for Christians (e.g. Sunday Schools, Fellowship Classes), and that she also offers a wide range of healthy community living for everyone (e.g. Youth Clubs, Pensioners Clubs, Young Wives Groups, etc. etc.). It is important that her own life is ordered efficiently and her money wisely spent, like any other well-run family.

To sum up, the Church exists both for worship and the endless task of proclamation-plus-service in the world. Especially her proclamations should come gently, her service never forgotten. When she is serving men, then she has established the right to be able to explain why she is doing so, and this enables her to talk about the gospel. Her inner life must be wholesome for the sake of all the tasks she is needed to do with Christ, not as an end in itself.

Every Christian is called to share in all this task. Nobody is exempt, however young, however old. Every Christian is called to share in the Church's worship, her service to mankind, and her explanation of why she does it and what she believes in. Within that whole task the individual Christian has a particular place, for God has a purpose for each individual life. There is a special place for you.

d. A MEMBER OF THE CHURCH

The Christian ought to become a member of the Church because he is committed to serving and obeying Christ, and the Church is the company of people who share together that commitment. He cannot manage without that company (to which, in the end, he owes his whole awareness of Christ). Neither can he manage to be faithful to Christ if he will not throw in his lot wholeheartedly with Christ's people.

Join up

Many people like to associate themselves with the Church's life (thank God), but demur at joining it wholly. Why? Sometimes because they do not like the notion of a public service at which they will be received (a thoroughly unworthy reason?), sometimes because a direct identification with the Church means that they are unable to stay aloof from her when she is being criticised, sometimes out of reluctance to accept the responsibilities of being a member and a fear that they will become too much involved in her life, sometimes because they reckon to be a member by virtue of their faith in Christ, whether or not that has been made formal. Are any of these reasons worthy of a Christian? It is almost like saying that one is in love with someone else but will not ratify it by marriage because that is a public service, it involves responsibilities, it indentifies one with that partner, or it is not necessary because the 'love' is everything. . . .

Rules

The rules of the Methodist Church regarding her membership are very simple. They are as follows:

1. All persons are welcomed into membership of The Methodist Church who sincerely desire to be saved from their sins through faith in the Lord Jesus Christ and evidence the same in life and conduct and who seek to have fellowship with Christ Himself and His people by taking up the duties and privileges of The Methodist Church.

2. It is the privilege and duty of Members of The Methodist Church to avail themselves of the two sacraments namely Baptism and the Lord's Supper. As membership of The

Methodist Church also involves fellowship it is the duty of all Members of The Methodist Church to seek to cultivate this in every possible way. The Weekly Class Meeting has from the beginning proved to be the most effective means of maintaining amongst Methodists true fellowship in Christian experience. All Members of The Methodist Church shall have their names entered on a Class Book, shall be placed under the pastoral care of a Class Leader, and shall receive a quarterly ticket of membership. They are also expected, as far as they are able, to contribute to the funds of the Church and to engage in some form of Christian service.

Not a party dress

The origin of the Class system, etc., will be explained shortly. But first a note must be recorded about the mood in which we contribute to the Church's life as members. At present the whole pattern of social life is changing very rapidly, the whole way in which we think, are educated, are entertained. In the midst of these rapid changes it is the inevitable responsibility of the Church to maintain certain permanent values, beliefs, and practices. The Christian faith is not a changeable commodity like a motor-car or party dress. It is good news about God's nature, which is everlastingly love and which is defined for us in the life, death and resurrection of Jesus Christ. There is a rock-like permanence at the centre of the faith because it is built upon Jesus Christ. Nothing can alter that.

Critics needed

But because Jesus is alive, He is constantly calling his people onwards into new expressions of obedience which will be appropriate to the new times in which we live. So there will be an on-going and constant development about the way in which we make our response to the living Christ, the words we use to speak about Him, the needs we discover that must now he met by Him, the wrongs that have freshly emerged all around us and must be reformed by Him. So the pattern of

Christian living will change, the form of the family life within the Church will change, the means of its service to the world will change.

In order to maintain the momentum of right change that the Church needs in order to keep faithful to the living Christ, she needs her members to be creative critics who hold with even greater tenacity to the bedrock foundation of the Church's life (her confession about Christ) whilst constantly exploring the new forms which He calls for. There is no value in being a sour critic, who can find no validity in any part of the life of God's family; there is little value in wanting things always to stay as they were fifty years ago (under the quite false impression that they were 'good old days'), but there is urgent need for the Church's members to be constantly pressing forward, developing new ways of responding to Christ. The Methodist constitution (as we shall shortly see) makes it possible for any member to be elected fairly quickly to those bodies within the Church's life where decisions are taken about her worship, her activities, her use of money. It is the urgent responsibility of each member to be the sort of creative critic who can make those bodies into lively ones in which the old is constantly revaluated, the stale is discarded, the new is experimented with, and the valuable is retained.

e. THE METHODIST CHURCH'S HISTORY

Early in the eighteenth century Samuel Wesley, an Anglican vicar in Epworth, Lincolnshire, raised a large family of ten children (eight others had died) despite constant poverty and thanks largely to the extraordinary powers of his wife. Two of his three sons (John and Charles) were especially gifted, made their way to Oxford and became learned clergymen. But they were appalled by the state of the Church at that time, the shallowness of much religion and the lack of concern for the great masses of poor people untouched by the care and faith of the Church. Together with some friends the Wesley brothers founded a 'Holy Club' of men who would lead a life of the strictest piety, learning and practical

Christian work. They were so methodical and meticulous that they were dubbed 'Methodists', a nickname which John gladly accepted and which was associated with his followers ever after.

A holy flop

In 1735, the brothers went as missionaries to Georgia, then one of the first colonies in North America. Charles soon returned, and John was an unfortunate flop. In 1738 he too was back in London, much shaken by his failures and by his own lack of simple, shining faith. He wrote: 'I went to America to convert the Indians; but oh! who shall convert me? . . . I have a fair summer religion . . . but let death look me in the face, and my spirit is troubled' (A reference to his terror when the ship was in a storm.) In May both brothers had profound religious experiences as a result of which both found deep, certain confidence that they personally were right with Christ, their sins were forgiven. He meant everything to them, and He would lead them into a life of total holiness.

God's super-men

The effects were tremendous. The two began a preaching activity that ranged the length and breadth of the land and over the seas. Everywhere they laboured to bring about a revival of genuine religion and to establish little 'societies' of believers, these societies to be part of the Parish Church's life. They were held together by a careful discipline and organisation to ensure that they would maintain a Christian behaviour and faith despite the grim conditions amongst the poor, and the frequent indifference of the local clergyman.

Charles was a highly effective preacher and an amazing poet. He is perhaps the greatest hymn-writer the Christian Church has yet been given. In no time, the Methodist Societies were being given magnificent hymns to sing to the liveliest tunes. John was a good preacher, courageous and of sturdy physique, a remarkable organiser, a strong-minded person who knew what he believed and brooked no opposition, a thinker of no mean ability, a writer who poured out sermons, tracts, letters, books, translations, instructions at astonishing speed.

A Church happens

Some support for their labour came from isolated vicars here and there, but steadily the Church of England and her bishops set their faces against this new force which took no notice of parish boundaries, sent men preaching everywhere (especially the open air), encouraged 'enthusiasm' and generally acted like new wine in an old bottle. Moreover Wesley was still vitally concerned about the new colonies in America, starved of preachers and crying out for missionaries. Because the Bishops would not ordain men and send them out, Wesley took the matter into his own hands in 1785, ordained men to the ministry and sent them. The final result was the birth of an extremely strong Methodist Church in America; the more immediate result was the estrangement of the Methodist societies from the Church of England.

Wesley organised every 'society' into a number of 'classes' under a Class Leader, the class meeting weekly to raise money, to share the experience of the Christian life and obtain instruction, to pray, and to plan its care for the members and the poor. Most societies soon built their own chapels. Wesley had many 'preachers' working full-time with him, some having been Anglican clergymen before, whereas others had simply been appointed by Wesley himself. These men travelled the length and breadth of the country on horseback, reading their books as they rode. Those who kept up their ordinary jobs and could not travel far afield were 'local preachers'. Gradually certain areas became more and more clearly defined in which the travels were more closely organised, these being known as 'Circuits'. Every year the preachers met with Wesley for an annual conference to review the work, plan ahead and give each other mutual encouragement.

Three Claims

There were three main assertions in the Methodist preaching:

1. Every man can be saved. This was in sharp contrast to the view widely held at the time that God only wished to save a certain section of mankind.
2. Every man can know that he is saved. This was in contrast to the prevailing atmosphere of religion, in which personal religious experience was played down.
3. Every man can be saved to the uttermost. This again was highly controversial, but Wesley consistently held up before his people the call of Christ to lead a life of perfect love (or scriptural holiness) and to be satisfied with nothing less.

See how they grow

Soon after Wesley's death in 1791, the Methodists finally became a separate Church, and the great evangelical revival in which the Wesleys had been key figures began to take new turns. In 1807, the revival broke out in new ways in the Potteries, but because the Wesleyan Methodists were now tightly organised under the strong rule of their ministers, this revival caused the birth of yet another Church—the Primitive Methodist Church, which spread like wildfire in the north of England especially. Other smaller Methodist bodies also resulted, but these were fused later into the United Methodist Church (from one of these bodies a minister named William Booth withdrew in 1865 to form the Salvation Army). In 1932, the three main bodies of Methodism were united to form out present Methodist Church.

All over the world as a result of the original revival, and also of subsequent missionary activity on the part of the home Church, Methodist Churches have come into existence. The Methodist Missionary Society is an integral part of our Church and every Church member is automatically a member. It began with a class meeting of slaves in the West Indies in 1760. In 1814 the Apostle of Methodist Missions, Dr Coke, after crossing the Atlantic eighteen times to preach in the U.S.A. and West Indies, died on board ship in the Indian Ocean on his way to Ceylon. In the same year, the Conference recommended the immediate establishment of a Methodist Missionary Society in every District in the Kingdom. But already the foundations of a great Church had been laid in America by Francis Asbury, an outstanding leader with many of Wesley's qualities. Today the Methodist Church is one of the largest Protestant bodies in the U.S.A.

The wide world o'er

For many years there have been Methodist Churches managing their own affairs in Ireland, Australia, New Zealand and South Africa. These were all Churches which were mainly composed of people of European ancestry. In 1961, they were joined by a new member of this world family—the Ghana Methodist Church which, except for the missionaries who continue to serve there, is almost wholly African in membership. Since then, the Methodist Church has become self-governing in Italy, Nigeria, Ceylon, Kenya, Sierra Leone. Today there is M.M.S. work in Europe, Africa, Ceylon, Burma, India, Hong Kong, South East Asia and the Caribbean, with over 550 missionaries helping to care for a Methodist Community of over 700,000. During the next few years, in rapid succession, many Methodist Districts overseas which are now part of the British Conference will become autonomous Methodist Churches.

There is also another way by which Churches become self-governing. In Canada, the Methodists joined with the Congregationalists and Presbyterians to form the United Church of Canada; in South India with the Anglicans too, to form the Church of South India, where over a hundred Methodist missionaries continue to serve and there are 400,000 Christians in the ex-Methodist areas of this great Church. Even where separate Methodist Conferences are born, the members of the Churches there look upon this kind of autonomy as a step towards a wider Church union. Whichever the way by which self-rule comes, the Church

Overseas looks to the mother Church to continue in partnership so that all may share each others' resources in offering the Gospel to the world. Ministers, doctors, teachers, nurses, agriculturalists, accountants and many others are needed urgently.

Millions and millions

For this partnership of men and materials about a million pounds is made available to the Church Overseas every year through the M.M.S. and our gifts are joined to over three million pounds raised overseas by the giving of the members and by government grants to hospitals and schools. Every member should take an intelligent interest in the whole Church and will find the Prayer Manual and the missionary magazines (The Kingdom Overseas and Women's Work) the best of helps.

The grand total of this world-wide evangelism is a Methodist Community of some 40,000,000 people, of whom over 19,000,000 are Church members (about 650,000 in the British Isles).

f. METHODISM—PART OF THE CHURCH UNIVERSAL

There is one family of all Christian people for whom Jesus Christ is Lord. The different communions (or Churches) are all members of this one body, all members of the One Holy, Catholic, Apostolic Church. In this connection we should note that 'catholic' means universal, embracing men of every nation. Methodists cherish their membership in this world family of Christian people. But the existence of the various communions is a constant puzzle, causing great perplexity and confusion. It can only be understood historically. The family tree below gives us the necessary outline:

1054—The Great Schism. From the fifth century onwards the two great centres of Church life—Rome in the West and Constantinople in the East—became more and more separated from each other. There were both theological and political reasons, and in 1054 the decisive split occurred.

Their two leaders (the Pope and the Patriarch) were not to meet again until 1967. The Eastern churches developed their own colourful forms of Church life and worship, called their Christianity 'orthodox', and became especially strong in Greece and Russia. Recently they have begun to share in the World Council of Churches.

From 1517 the Reformation broke up the Western Church. Throughout the Middle Ages it had veered further away from the New Testament pattern despite the reforming work of St Francis in the 13th Century. The major reform broke out through the determination and tremendous theological ability of Martin Luther and was assisted both by the desire of many European states to shake themselves free from any subservience to the Pope and by the whole new awakening in thought and culture which we now call 'The Renaissance'.

Luther and Calvin

Luther called men back to the central theme of the New Testament, that we are saved by faith in Christ and can do nothing to earn special favour with God. He called men back to find their faith offered them through the Bible, rather than the traditions of the Church. The resulting reformation saw the birth of various patterns of Protestant Church in different lands. In Switzerland (Geneva) John Calvin published the first major work on Protestant doctrine (*The Institutes of the Christian Religion*) and re-organised the Church's life so that laymen were given a key role. The 'Reformed' Churches are the result, the (Presbyterian) Church of Scotland being one of them.

Those who remained loyal to Rome and the authority of the Pope are termed 'Roman Catholics'. The Church of England was reformed by being loosed from obedience to the Pope in Rome, by re-ordering her worship according to a new Prayer Book, and by discarding many of the more superstitious doctrines. Yet she retained bishops to govern her life, and thereby showed that she still wished to retain links with the historic Catholic Church.

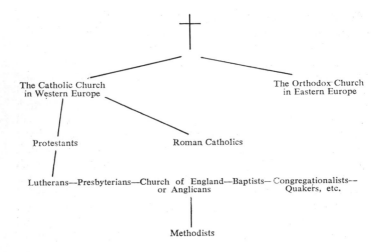

The Catholic Church in Western Europe — The Orthodox Church in Eastern Europe

Protestants — Roman Catholics

Lutherans—Presbyterians—Church of England—Baptists— Congregationalists—— or Anglicans — Quakers, etc.

Methodists

A Free Church

Methodism, as we have seen, sprang out of the Church of England. She has always shown many marks of her parentage —for example, our present Communion Service has been that used by the Church of England. But in other ways she has always found herself in sympathy with other bodies originating in the Reformation (e.g. the Baptists and Congregationalists). These were never officially recognised as the religion of the State as was the Church of England. This meant that they were denied many privileges, but were left free to order their own life and worship and ministry. The Church of England, being an 'established' Church, is not totally free from government control, and enjoys a certain status and privilege in return. Methodism has always been a 'Free Church', with its own Conference able to order its life, its worship and its ministry.

That they all may be one

The Ecumenical Movement is the name given to the whole process whereby all the Christian Churches have grown steadily closer to each other in understanding and affection over the last fifty years. It really began in a conference of missionaries in Edinburgh in 1910, but the most important agency for helping it forward has been the World Council of Churches, born in 1949 in Amsterdam. Methodism has always been a very keen member of the World Council. She has become more and more convinced that God is calling the Churches into unity so that the Church will be like the New Testament pattern, and so that it will be able to do far more for Christ. Hence Methodists have been willing to enter into union schemes all over the world, and are now deeply involved in negotiations with the Church of England in this country. We should rejoice that since Pope John XXIII and the Vatican Council, which he called to refashion the life of the Roman Catholic Church, a new spirit has been generated amongst Roman Catholics, and they now take a keen interest in the life and faith of Protestants.

Easter 1980?

In a momentous Conference in Nottingham in 1964 the Protestant Churches in our country were called upon to covenant together 'to work and pray for a united Church to be inaugurated by an agreed date. We dare to hope that this date should be not later than Easter Day 1980.' It is too early to predict what will happen to this intention, but already some schemes are well advanced, such as the Anglican-Methodist one. Meanwhile it is our duty to try to do together with other Churches the many things in which we share a common interest, and only to do separately those things which involve deep matters of belief or custom.

This means that certain very special qualities are required from the Christian today in his relationships with other Christians from other communions and backgrounds. Whereas in the past we found it possible to be 'Methodists', and to devote our time to trying to enter more and more fully into our own particular heritage and to furthering the life of our own particular denomination, it is clear that the new ecumenical era in which we live requires different qualities.

It requires from us a tremendous respect for Christians from other communions, a major effort from us to understand them and their ways, a persistent working to draw us closer together and to share more and more of our Church life with them, and a readiness to give up some cherished practices that are no longer important in the new Church to which Christ is bringing us.

g. METHODIST ORGANISATION

Every Methodist Church is termed a 'Society' and has its life directed by two bodies, the Leaders Meeting and the Trustees. The latter are especially responsible for the building itself, its upkeep and repair and use. They are a legal body with special legal powers in relation to the property. The Leaders are responsible for the life of the Church, its worship, its care for its members, its organisations, its finances, its work for the neighbourhood. The key officers of the Church have a place in that meeting (e.g. Society Stewards, Sunday School Superintendent, etc.), but all the members of that Society elect representatives to serve annually in the ratio of one per thirty members. This election takes place at the Annual Society Meeting, when it is every member's duty to attend. Those representatives must be at least eighteen years old and must have been members for at least two years.

Circuits and Plans

But every Church is a member of a 'Circuit' or grouping of Churches. The Circuit is a grouping which shares a lot of its money together and organises its life together. In particular, the Ministers are all servants of the Circuit, which will decide which Churches they are to watch over. The main Circuit meeting which handles all its finances and policy is the Quarterly Meeting, to which every Leader and Trustee is entitled to go. This is chaired by a senior Minister (the 'Superintendent'), who is also responsible for deciding who shall lead every service in the Churches in this Circuit and who has this published in the 'Circuit plan'. This grouping means that strong Churches are constantly able to help weaker ones, and arrangements can always be made to ensure that every Church however small has a Minister to work with it, even if he has several Churches under his care.

The Circuits in every region are grouped together into 'Districts', which are roughly the size of a large county. They have a senior Minister (known as the 'Chairman') to watch over them, and have two special District meetings per year, known as 'Synods'. To govern the whole life of the Church throughout the country, the Church holds a 'Conference' every summer, of 650/700 members, half laymen and women, half ministers, some ex-officio, the majority elected by the Synods. The Methodist Conference has complete authority over the life of the Church, over its ministers and organisations, and is the governing body of all its affairs. It is presided over by a Minister elected annually, known as the 'President', who therefore represents the whole Methodist Church during his year of office.

How Methodism is run

THE CONFERENCE
Some 700, half Ministers, half laymen, over whom the President of the Conference presides for ten days in
June.

/ | \

34 DISTRICTS with Synods
of all the Ministers and many laymen meeting in May and September over which the Chairmen of the Districts preside.

/ | \

Some **800 CIRCUITS** or groups of churches with a Quarterly Meeting over which the Superintendent Minister presides.

/ | \

Some **10,000 CHURCHES,** big and little, including **YOURS.**

Tasks galore

Because the Methodist Church has wide responsibilities, it has a number of 'Departments' set up to manage certain important aspects of its life, and to report every year to the Conference. These have a full-time staff (usually in London) and are normally headed by ministers set aside for the purpose. The largest is the Methodist Missionary Society, responsible for helping our overseas work with men, money and advice, and for keeping up a regular liaison with other Methodist Churches overseas. The Home Mission Department is responsible for promoting evangelistic work in this country and for meeting special needs which require the Church's concern (e.g. work in prisons or the Forces). The Chapel Department watches over all our buildings, their planning and financing. The Youth Department helps the Church in all aspects of youth work (Sunday School work, Youth Club work, etc.), the Local Preachers Department watches over the training and equipping of its Local Preachers, and the Christian Citizenship Department is responsible for expressing the Church's judgment on every vital social issue, to train and educate the Church, and to speak on its behalf. The Ministerial Training Department trains all our ministers, the Education Department watches over the many Methodist schools (of which 9 are Public Schools) and the two Teacher Training Colleges.

In addition to these Departments, there are many organisations which were set up to carry out specific tasks by the Church, and they must also report annually to the Conference. These include the National Children's Home, the Wesley Deaconess Order, the Epworth Press (originally founded by John Wesley), Methodist Homes for the Aged, and Methodist International Houses. There are also specific committees to deal with matters like Church Membership, the Church in industry, Healing, the care of Immigrants, Radio and Television, Religious Drama, Stewardship, etc.

More or less democratic

Most of the Departments have persons in each District and Circuit (and sometimes in each Society) who will help to further their work and to keep the whole Church alive to particular issues and concerns. Thus there is a Youth Secretary in every Church and Circuit and District, similarly an Overseas Missions Secretary, and so on.

This organisation is constantly being reviewed and adapted, and in smaller Churches it is often very much simplified. It is a democratic system. A member of a Leaders Meeting can be elected to the District Synod, and then to the Conference if he or she has been a member of the Methodist Church for at least five years. A Quarterly Meeting can send a request to Conference (on any matter whatever, known as a 'memorial') and the whole Conference is bound to make a suitable reply and inform the Circuit of its judgment.

References

56. 1 Corinthians 3,10,11.
57. 1 Corinthians 1,22-24;15,3-7.
58. 1 Peter 2,9.
59. Ephesians 2,10; John 14,12.
60. An interesting example is in the hymns of the early Church, extracts from which occur in Revelation. See 4, 8-11; 5,9,12,13; 7,10,12; 15, 3,4.
61. Matthew 28,19; I Corinthians 11,23-26.
62. Romans 6,4; 1 Peter 3,21.
63. Acts 19,4-6; 1 Corinthians 12,13; Titus 3,5.
64. Acts 16,15,33.
65. Acts 2,41.
66. Acts 2,46;20,7; 1 Corinthians 10,16.
67. Luke 4,18,19.

4. Assumptions we have been making

THROUGHOUT this Manual so far we have been making extensive assumptions, and have never paused to take a good look at them. We have assumed, for example, that when the Bible stresses a particular interpretation of some issue, then we ought to accept it as the correct one. We have assumed that Jesus was no mere man but must be viewed in bigger ways altogether. We have assumed that the teaching of the Church down through the centuries has a particular authority for us now, even if the Church has almost always been deeply divided on various matters. We have assumed that there is a vital place within our life of faith for the steady use of critical reason, and a place for us simply to kneel before God and humbly accept His truth.

We must look more closely at all these assumptions. This closer look is what we mean by 'theology' (right thinking about God and His ways with men). Every Christian is called to know, and be interested in, theology. It is this alone which makes us able to give a good account of the faith we live by.

a. ASSUMPTIONS ABOUT GOD

The Christian assumes to begin with that there is a basic sense and plan and regularity running right through the whole universe, as a result of which we can discover many laws which describe how the universe functions. The scientist is the expert in discovering these laws and principles. But he can only do his work by making the same assumption that Christians make—that the universe is not a meaningless jumble of wild forces, but has a certain plan running right through it all. Every scientific advance makes this more and more reasonable.

God and Evolution

Christians then believe that this is due to the universe having been made by one Planner who patterned it all and established the laws and principles upon which it would develop, who built into it the sequence which we call 'evolution', and who must have made the whole out of nothing. Perhaps that is not the best way to express it—rather, the Planner made the whole thing out of his own intense desire to create, his will, his joy in having more in existence than simply himself. Christians believe that the most appropriate word to describe the Planner is 'God', and that since He has this will to create things we are almost bound to think of Him as a 'person'. We ourselves, in a puny and petty way, have an inkling of what it means to be a 'person', to have a will of our own and be able to use it. Nevertheless, just as the Creator is of a different order from what is created, so God is more than a 'person', and this is just what the doctrine of the Holy Trinity, described earlier in this manual, declares.

More than a Person

But thirdly, Christians believe that this person, God, is one who wishes to show us what He is like, wishes to communicate with us, wishes to create a bond of love with us. This is not a further great leap of faith because anyone who has a creative urge within him is a person who wishes to show himself to others. If I long to paint, my handiwork will express something of my own personality in such a way that others also get a glimpse of it. So too, if God is the Creator, that must mean that He longs to show His own nature to others, He is a 'revealing' God. It must mean that the universe does also show us something about Him. As the Psalmist puts it:

'The heavens are telling the glory of God
And the firmament proclaims his handiwork' (Psalm 19, 1).

A great many of the arguments we have about 'God' would be much clearer and more profitable if Christians made it plain that they work on these three assumptions. You have to make *some* assumptions like this before you can discuss life at all, just as you have to find some place upon which to site a camera before you can take any picture whatever of anything. That Christians share the first major assumption with every scientist is a clear indication that there is no basic conflict between 'science' and Christianity. Many scientists cannot follow up by making the second assumption with us, but many can—and there are many, many people who wish that they could, and who look with wistful longing upon those whose belief in God gives so much more certainty with which to deal with life. A Christian who can talk clearly to such people about his faith is at once a useful evangelist.

b. ABOUT THE BIBLE
The belief that God is a revealing God immediately raises the question, 'Very well, where and how does He reveal himself?' We have already hinted that He inevitably reveals something of His nature in the sort of world He has made, just as an artist reveals something of his personality in every painting that he paints. No painting quite manages to reveal *everything* about the artist. So the world that God has made reveals some truth about Him—His orderliness, His steadiness, His vastness (the universe is a very large one . . .) His wisdom which is way beyond our capacity to understand. Some Christians go much further and say that the universe shows us God's love because of the beauty of the world, the provision He makes for us, etc. etc. But there are serious difficulties about such a further step, since there are very many ugly features in the world (earthquakes, for example), and very many people who are starving, or subject to disease and disaster. If we wish to talk about God's love, we must find some other justification for it. But whilst we can find

in the world (as God has created it) many clear indications of His purpose and nature, this alone does not lead us to know Him as fully as Christian faith indicates. How can we take this further step?

Chosen people

Christians believe that God took hold of a particular people, the Jews, and used their experience to reveal His nature. There was no favouritism about this, since it was a dramatic, costly, often terrifying experience for them. It was intended to be one which would enable them to speak to the whole world, not one for their own pet benefit. But they rebelled time and time again against it. They often wished they had never been selected for such an ordeal, but had been left alone to their own devices. The Old Testament is the record of what happened, of how God showed something of His nature through His dealings with the Jews. He showed especially that He was a 'saving' God who wanted to lift men out of the mess into which our selfishness and blindness puts us.

When the time was ripe, and the Jewish people had been prepared by long, hard centuries, God took the crucial plunge. He revealed His own magnificent love towards men by demonstrating this in one special man, one chosen agent, His own 'Son', Jesus of Nazareth. The New Testament is the record of what happened, and the impact this had upon people of the time like John, Paul, Peter, James who wrote their letters to explain the significance of this great act of God, the consequence of this fact of Jesus for *our* lives.

Not infallible

The Bible is, therefore, the record of God's most vital dealings with us. Our knowledge of God is knowledge which we acquire as a result of the events which the Bible relays to us. Without the Bible account, we would know very little about God and would be left to our own imaginings. This is why the Bible is the one prime source-book for Christian faith. It is not an infallible book in that every word is so dictated by God that it is perfectly accurate. Because it was written by men, it has the inevitable marks of men's authorship upon it—the writers had all the limitations of their own particular period of history (e.g. the early ones write as if the world is flat because that is what everyone then believed[68]), they sometimes got minor details wrong (e.g. Matthew will describe an event involving two men and Jesus, Mark describes the same event as only involving one man and Jesus[69]), they wrote according to the stage which God's teaching process had reached with them (e.g. the early ones believed that God preferred to exist on the tops of mountains[70] or that he wanted them to slaughter all their enemies[71]) or they wrote using thought-forms that may seem strange and unnatural to us (e.g. God is thought of as sitting on a throne surrounded by cherubim and seraphim,[72] or with hosts of angels playing harps and clad in white).[73]

The Bible is a library of books, written at different periods and often from different standpoints. Sometimes a book will be straightforward history, sometimes it will include legends of long ago, sometimes it will be poetry and myth, sometimes it will be describing the life and preaching of a great man of God, sometimes it will be a letter written to some congregation in the early Church. Whatever the form of the book, whoever the writer, whatever the period of its origin, it is setting out part of the amazing process whereby God has shown himself to men—and it is this that gives it its worth and authority. The word of God is at the heart of it.

c. ABOUT JESUS

Christians believe that Jesus of Nazareth was the 'Son of God'. This needs a closer look. It does not mean that Jesus was a freak who could not really be called a 'man' at all. On the contrary, the Bible makes it clear that He was fully human. He grew up like any other child, dependent upon His parents and maturing steadily as the years passed.[74] He shared in the life of a big (and very poor) family with lots of sisters and brothers.[75] He learnt a trade and for many

61

years practised it. He enjoyed the company of women[76]; indeed, He enjoyed all human company, both that of the good people as much as that of the bad and the social outcasts.[77] He scandalised the straight-laced religious folk by His presence at the parties staged by the more dubious characters of Palestine.[78] He had a subtle sense of humour which often comes out in His teaching when He pictures the grotesque.[79] He grew tired and hungry.[80] He could be deeply moved,[81] even to tears.[82] There were some people with whom He felt a special intimacy and who became His closest friends.[83] He was, then, fully human. Indeed, if we want to know what it is to be a *real* man, we must look at Jesus because He is the only real man who has ever lived.

'The only begotten Son'

But this by no means does justice to Him. He was utterly sure that He had a quite unique standing with God,[84] and this was the key to the whole of His life, His teaching, His activity. He believed that God was uniquely at work through Him,[85] so He did not deny the term 'Messiah' when applied to Him,[86] and normally referred to Himself as 'son of man'.[87] His complete openness to the powers of God resulted in capacity to heal, which appears to us to be miraculous,[88] capacity to understand people which defies explanation,[89] capacity to suffer hardship and yet offer forgiveness which leaves us breathless.[90] His life was lived in such vivid awareness of the presence and the will of God that everyone sensed God whenever Jesus came near.[91]

It was Jesus' resurrection from the dead that enabled the early Christians to see Him in full perspective. He was the supreme revealer of God, demonstrating to the full the total out-going love and concern of God for all people.[92] He was God's victorious power to save mankind displayed freely for all to see, the agent of God's mastery over death as well as life.[93] He is now the Head over all creation.[94] The more the early Christians thought about Him, the more they realised that He must have been with God from the very beginning[95] (for God did not suddenly change or get bigger when Jesus appeared on earth), that He must have been God's agent in creating the world as well as saving it,[96] and that He would be God's agent for completing His whole purpose at the end of all things.[97] So it was inevitable that Jesus came to be worshipped and adored and loved in the same way as God the Father is worshipped and adored and loved. To see Jesus is to see God.[98] To love Jesus is to love God. To worship Jesus is to worship God.

d. ABOUT MAN AND HIS DESTINY

The Christian believes that each and every man is like Adam, a 'child of God',[99] uniquely made by and for God— yet no man's life ever works out quite right. It is never a steady development of pure love for God and man. It is a muddle, with love for self tangled up with love for God, with self-interest and self-concern bungling his love for man. The Christian expresses this by saying that man is a sinner.[100] Sin is our 'missing the mark', falling down on the purpose God has for us,[101] refusing His way for our lives and disobeying His will.[102] Every man can realise it most clearly by contrasting his life with that of Christ, whereupon his looks dreadful, or at least tawdry, twisted, second-rate.[103]

It is the will of God that every man should be rescued from this mess and brought to full perfection and maturity, made like Christ, living spontaneously in complete obedience to God.[104] The rescue began with the crucial event of Jesus Christ, His life and death and resurrection.[105] It proceeds within our lives as we grow 'in Christ', trusting and obeying and living for Him.

Death, and then?

Within this purpose of God death has a clear place. Death frees us from the physical bodies which are inevitably subject to frailty, decay and limitation. Death provides God with the opportunity to give us new 'bodies' which are no longer corruptible.[106] Every man must go through death, must face up to Christ afterwards (which is what we mean by 'Judgement Day')[107] and must find full bliss by a complete response to Him (which is what we mean by 'heaven')[108] or final nothing by rejecting Him ('Hell').[109] Heaven, then, is to be at perfect peace within the glory of God's everlasting love and energy. Hell is to turn one's back upon Him and is quite impossible to imagine or describe, yet the Bible makes it clear that it is still a terrible possibility.[110]

The world's end

But while we can contemplate the destiny of human life by considering what happens to each individual, there is another more biblical way of looking at it. The Bible is mainly concerned with *all* mankind and *all* creation. It teaches clearly that just as God created the world in the begining out of nothing, because He chose to, so He will complete His purpose for it one day.[111] He will work through Jesus Christ, will finally establish the kingdom of God, will purge all creation of its sin and pain and decay, will perfectly make all things new.[112] This is the ultimate state towards which all mankind and all world history moves, whether the world has realised it or not.

It is this certainty of a good purpose running right through all existence which enables the Christian to have a special type of optimism, to persevere in doing good despite all discouragements, to face death soberly, to be upheld by a permanent hope.[113] He knows that the whole world lies under God's control and ever will. For him the classic demonstration of this is the Great Fact of Jesus Christ.

e. THE CREED

The first tremendous event which followed upon Jesus' transformation to be with God, and no longer confined to a human body, was the gift of the Holy Spirit. The early followers suddenly experienced the power of Jesus at work within their own lives even more startlingly and energetically than when Jesus was walking beside them. It was as if He had been re-born within them, bringing all sorts of power and vitality. They believed that this was the gift which Jesus had called 'the Holy Spirit' and about which prophets had written and John the Baptist had preached. At first they had no distinction between 'the Spirit of God', 'the Spirit of Jesus' and 'the Holy Spirit',[114] and only did they talk clearly of the Holy Spirit when they had realised that this was a more precise use of words.

Summing it all up

After this, they began to work out all the consequences of belief in Jesus and the Holy Spirit. The New Testament is one result. But in time it became useful to summarise all the major things that Christians held to be the truth about God and His dealings with us. The Creeds are the result. Here is the Apostles Creed:

> I believe in God the Father Almighty,
>   Maker of heaven and earth.
> And in Jesus Christ His only Son our Lord
>   Who was conceived by the Holy Ghost
>   Born of the virgin Mary
>   Suffered under Pontius Pilate
>   Was crucified, dead and buried
>   He descended into hell
>   The third day He rose again from the dead
>   He ascended into heaven
>   And sitteth on the right hand of God the
>   Father Almighty.
>   From thence He shall come to judge the
>   quick and the dead.
> I believe in the Holy Ghost
>   The holy Catholic Church
>   The communion of saints
>   The forgiveness of sins
>   The resurrection of the body
>   And the life everlasting.

Amen.

The Creed is not laid down as a body of truth which every Christian must accept, whether he understands it or not. It is a summary of those things which Christians have found to be true. It may be phrased in a manner which requires

65

very thorough explanation and re-phrasing before we can grasp what is involved, and can put it into terms which make the most sense for us today. But it is treasured by the Church as an outline of the full consequence of Christian belief. It is hoped that every Methodist will find that it outlines what the Church has helped him to discover to be true.

References

68. The earth has 'ends' as in Isaiah 40,28 or Psalm 19,4.
69. Compare Mark 5,1-20 with Matthew 8,28-9,1.
70. Exodus 19,3.
71. 1 Samuel 15,32,33; Psalm 137,9.
72. Isaiah 6.
73. Revelation 5,8;7,9.
74. Luke 2,51,52.
75. Mark 6,3.
76. Luke 10,38-42.
77. Matthew 11,19.
78. Luke 19,7.
79. Matthew 23,24;7,3.
80. Mark 4,38; Luke 24,41.
81. Mark 6,34;1.41.
82. Luke 19,41; John 11,35.
83. Mark 9,2-8; John 21,15-22.
84. Matthew 11,27; John 14,6.
85. Luke 11,20; John 5,36.
86. Mark 8,29; Matthew 26,64.
87. Mark 10,45; John 5,27.
88. Mark 9,25-29; John 9,1-12.
89. Mark 10,17-22; John 4,16-18,29.
90. Luke 23,34.
91. Mark 1,24;15,39.
92. Colossians 2,9.
93. Romans 8,35-39.
94. Ephesians 1,20-23.
95. 1 John 1,1-4; 1 Peter 1,19,20.
96. Colossians 1,16,17; Hebrews 1,2.
97. 1 Corinthians 15,20-28.
98. John 14,9.
99. Genesis 1,27.
100. Luke 18,13; 1 John 1,8.
101. Romans 3,23.
102. Romans 7,19,20; Colossians 1,21.
103. Luke 5,8; John 8,7-9.
104. John 12,32; 1 Timothy 2,4,5.
105. Matthew 1,21; Colossians 1, 13,14.
106. John 3,16; Philippians 3,21.
107. Matthew 25,31-46; Romans 14,10.
108. John 14,3; Revelation 7,9,10.
109. Matthew 13,47-50; 2 Peter 2,17.
110. Luke 13,22-27.
111. 1 Peter 1,3-5.
112. 2 Peter 3,13; Revelation 21, 1-5.
113. John 16,33; 1 Corinthians 15,58.
114. e.g. Romans 8,9-11.

Conclusion

'Now to him who is able to do immeasurably more than we can ask or conceive, by the power which is at work among us, to him be glory in the Church and in Christ Jesus from generation to generation evermore. Amen' (Ephesians 3,20-21).

References

115. Ephesians 3,20,21.